THE DARK'S HUMMING

Megan Merchant

GLASS LYRE PRESS

Copyright © 2017 Megan Merchant

Paperback ISBN: 978-1-941783-32-0

All rights reserved: except for the purpose of quoting brief passages for review, no part of this book may be reproduced or transmitted in any form or by any means, electronic or mechanical, including photocopying, recording, or by any information storage and retrieval system, without permission in writing from the publisher.

Cover art: © Grietpearl | Dreamstime.com
Author Photo:
Design & layout: Steven Asmussen
Copyediting: Linda E. Kim

Glass Lyre Press, LLC
P.O. Box 2693
Glenview, IL 60025
www.GlassLyrePress.com

Acknowledgments

I would like to extend gratitude to the editors and journals who first published versions of these poems:

"Grass Stars":   *Doll Hospital*, Issue Two

"How to Snare a Wandering Womb":   *The Offbeat*, March 2015

"Melancholy"   *Doll Hospital*, Forthcoming

"Pen Pal, Asylum":   *Thrush*. January, 2015

"Prairie Madness":   *The Offbeat*, March 2015

"Prayer for the Sick":   *Rat's Ass Review*, Summer 2015

"Tall Pines":   *Bodega : Online*, 2015

"Warning":   *Doll Hospital*, Forthcoming

"Winter":   Eber & Wein Publishing

CONTENTS

Acknowledgments	iii

I

Melancholy	1
Have You Ever	2
Urban Bird	3
Grass Stars	4
Second Child	6
Household Labor	7
Cutting the Cord	8
The Lying-In Room	9
Newborn	10

II

Warning	13
A Faucet of Lilacs	16
Unfit	17
Mama's Little Helper	18
Infirmary for Nervous Diseases	20
I Sold The Play-Kitchen While You Were Asleep.	23
Postpartum Blues	24
Decomposition	26
Common Room	27

II (CONT'D)

How to Snare a Wandering Womb	28
Dogwood	30
In the Waiting Room of the Earth Clinic	31
Pen Pal, Asylum	32
Diagnosis	34
Prairie Madness	35

III

In the Light of Morning	41
Harbinger	42
I Want to be Thrilled	43
Sickness	44
Tall Pines	45
My Son Shakes a Small Rainmaker	46
I Offer You This	47
Building a Life from Sorrow	49
On Your Sixth Birthday	50
Elegy, Exhale	51
Little One	52
Prayer for the Sick	53
Mothering	55
Two-Lane Road, Tree	56
Winter	57
About the Author	59

For my children, who add magic into this world with every breath. For the man who gave me the tall pines and endless days of *yes*. For the editors and staff at Glass Lyre Press, who gave these poems a home where compassion, integrity, and kindness matter. With gratitude ...

I

Melancholy

They call the wasp
an inclusion—wingless,
black, bent in iridescent
resin the color of burnished
light that weeps through
tempered glass across
a winter floor.

A fragile symphony
wrapped in decades
of hardening.

Have You Ever

seen lilacs in a flood,
    a bird wince,
        a splinter floating
            in a cracked cup of water,

slept on the recent earth-mound
    of a grave, hitched a ride with a man
        who kept his hand on your thigh
            until you whispered *Kentucky*,

felt glass slicing the sharp arch
    of your foot, the way the gas station
        attendant pulled it free,
            how quickly your blood mixed
                with the oil and tar of his hands?

Kiss me like that,
    with an echo waiting
        in the spate of your mouth.

Lay your body open,
    touch each scar slowly as a feather
        falling from a wing.

Urban Bird

I've nested a bird's cradle of needles, a cup-shape woven with gossamer
thread, apron strings, seasoned twigs, a knot-hole in a splintered branch
that leans over our garden gate.

He said, *be warm like June. Mother them. Sing until they hatch.*
My body, a larking heat lamp. My body, a hymn lashed into dark.
Even moss grows on gravestones living off nothing but air.

But the eggs never fractured, the eggs never pipped.
They hollowed, they dried.
Empty as begging, thin as a filament of prayer.

I buried them in the corner, shifted dirt until my hands blackened,
like a dog digging a tunnel, knowing nothing about the other side,
scampering to catch the fading smell of home that's carried by the wind.

Grass Stars

I was pregnant in a patchwork dress
and the day shivered yellow, as if I were
concealing a secret that could unravel an entire
field of grass stars. I was faultless.

Then I burst and we fell into these stuck places.
I read and read but speaking came hard when
walls were the only texture and people's voices
forgot to remind me I was something other
than a charcoal-etched list, a tender honey-do.

An udder. The baby coos cuteness and need.
We dance by the night window until she
forgets to cry. I whisper the kinds of sadness
splayed in the news and she sleeps.

If I never set her down, her dreams will
prepare her for this world, how to always
flourish in motion. How to crave lightness,
death. I am busy being her cradle.

When I glued the cat's paws to the floor,
it wasn't out of spite for its constant *yowl*,
its pathetic heat. I just couldn't be another
post to rub against, another fixture in these
rooms.

The doctor says my sadness can be bright.
The way berries plump under the burnt crust.
They swell and glisten. He says there's a little
pill that can make the world go from harried
and dumb to air-crisped and floaty.

A full bottle could make me kind.

I light the stove and crave its warmth,
its thick lullaby that swims and swims
and swallows my lungs.

Second Child

How can I explain?

The other day it rained,
drawing earthworms from our lawn

and I missed
a doctor's appointment

because I refused to step outside—
the tenderness of their bodies

sprawled along concrete, slippery,
frail, each with five

beating hearts.

Household Labor

The creak of the cupboard opening,
the smack of the cupboard closing.

The wood grain scratching, the gold latch un-latching,
the fit-key turning in the chest.

The push-breath of the door widening,
the shut-breath of the door narrowing.

The slip-knot silk unwinding,
the slip-knot silk retying.

The taut bow pulling, the fletching grazing.
The taut bow snapping, the shaft soaring.

The womb like a trembling animal.
The womb like an animal wandering the trembling dark.

Cutting the Cord

If the cord is cut too close,
he'll be cursed with a tiny soldier
that, even at full attention,
cannot rise tall enough
for the affair.

Too long, and he'll be shunned
from tucking it fully into any
wet socket. He'll know only
partial pleasure.

Please, cut the blood-wet
line that still beats
at a hardy mark.

Let it snake and retreat
between my thighs.

Let it be a purple-veined
hummingbird wing

that sings by flapping
back, back, back.

The Lying-In Room

Recognize death like paper walls,
the rain and haze condensing on windows.

From outside, you can't see the soul
of what's walking around, dazed in underwear.

Inside, there's a disquiet, a thin wail, a surrender.

You think it's coming from
the wood slats,
or the roof tiles crying under the weight of it.

But it's not.
So you keep bumping into

counters
and corners that haven't shifted in years,

not because of the dark's humming, but because
you've lost the feel for air—taut and fluid at once,

swimming in the static all around.

Newborn

His fevered cry rises like rosemary dough
throughout the house—astringent, hoarse,
unaffected by binding his body to my breast,
rubbing his back and legs with oil.

I ask my grandmother's ghost for the leaves
and vines she dried on the kitchen table
when I was little and blistered, still deciding
how long to stay.

Oregano for a toothache, warm-pressed
olive oil in ears, a cracked egg underneath the bed
to ward off dark dreams, but I've long forgotten
the dialect of newborn suffering.

I work circles around his calves and thighs, worried
he was born with my hue of anger—the kind that stunts
roots, makes them recoil from barbing
into the just-tilled earth.

II

Warning

I inherited a color,
gray, and a gene
that frays once
a baby arrives.

As a child, I prepared,
painted every surface cyan,
kept jars of indigo beads
in the window, learned
a slow waltz I could do
at the lip of the hospital
roof, gown flapping
like a flag.

My facility
was named after
a saint,
smelled of sulfur
and cotton,
fresh pairs of orange
traction socks
to keep from slipping
on the always
just-washed floor.

It's an imbalance,
they explained,

so surely I'd fall
at the lip of anything,
or shift
into the place
of lead and ash.

My grandmother
is the only
one I know
who
escaped,

her hair,
brilliant white,

turned early
and has refused
to fade

even as
her body
continues to shrink
into sleep-filled days.

When
I lean in
to give her a kiss,
she whispers
that the light is
too bright.

I'm not sure
if she is talking
about the musty
daylight
filtering through
the covered
window,

or speaking
to the sepia
ghosts that
adorn her walls.

When I turn
to leave,
she squints,
as if behind
a windshield,
driving headlong
into the sun.

A Faucet of Lilacs

They said her wrists
were a faucet
of lilacs,

and all around
her, particles of dander
and wisps

of hair danced
in a line of sun,
illuminating

the shape
her body made
on horizontal slats
of the floor.

Unfit

It's easy to love the imperfection of us;
it can be named—

cracked tiles, sprouting weeds,
gray fuzz glazing the bread,

saying hurtful things at the train
terminal when neither one

holds a ticket. It's easier to let
sorrow board alongside strangers,

drive home unpacked, clean.
Closed doors were never our passion.

We do ugly out loud,
as if the damage isn't complete without a witness.

But we're different now.
Polite, even, in our anger.

Perfect
as the ruby scar along the line

of my belly that divides. A disquiet that
only a mother can hear,

about how I've traded lust for a love
you're sure I'll ruin.

Mama's Little Helper

This little pill
is a pile of dirty mouths
and dishes,

carpools and roasted
dinners at five,

the news-wrapped fish
scale-cold in the fridge.

How long will it take
to thin out the pinched-white

bones, see if the coursing stream
still floats in gaze-glassed eyes?

This little pill is your Sears catalog,
your steam that eases wrinkles flat,

the walls you've hammered
and hung,

the wood clock that stutters
two minutes before nine.

Ten years of misplaced seconds.
Welcome home. Wipe your feet.

This little pill tells
the wryest jokes,
clears the table,
runs a bath,

puts the kids to bed early,
makes it easy with a smile,
It's okay.
You've had a rough day.
Relax.

I've got this.

And when the alone-at-last hush
coats the room, we sip day-stories
from each other's cups.

This little pill dutifully swallows
your words,
makes them bounce, a racquetball game with socks.

I'm careful to skirt and say *new wallpaper,*
shattered mixing bowl, sharper knitting
needle,

so when the day arrives and you're
asked to describe what's missing,

you'll look around with care,
glimpse the polished portrait
over the mantel,
add my married name
as inventory,

polite as starched sheets
on a rainy day.

Infirmary for Nervous Diseases

I.

They are scooping
my ovaries free
with a tin spoon.

They are sealing
them in a floating jar,
a glass sea of formaldehyde.

Abcdefg ...
Count backwards.

The nurses keep nodding
for me to rest,
their eyes are harpooning
hours ahead of me,
their needles are pointed at my head.

They firm the sheets,
they are always firming the sheets
with their neat little hands,
wedding bands cold as stars.

Their starched white caps
wear a woven band

like a strip of blood-wet
cloth laid over the eyes of the dead.

The doctor says I spent too many
hours sewing with a machine,

that each time the barbed needle
pierced the cloth, grabbed the thread,

the vibration left a loop in my spine,
the vibration shuttered my uterus
into hiding, flapping
hysterically
in the blood cavity
of my body.

They will glue it
into place, scold the rest
with a knife.

II.

The nurses bring
a palette of soft foods,
they greedily swallow
my alphabet.

When I ask for my purse,
I can no longer
pull rouged words
to explain how
even the day-stretch of dreams
are blank waves
pouring out of a kitchen faucet,
dirty steak knife lying in wait,
jar of pimientos
glowing above the sink.

The only thing I can think to say is
*my husband takes his martini with
two olives.*

I Sold The Play-Kitchen While You Were Asleep.

When you woke, you climbed inside the shadow-

shape its absence left and laid your tiny body

long, as if to say *I know someday you too*

will leave me.

Postpartum Blues

It's a lullaby we sing in the dark.
It floats around the edges of the room

and clamps my mouth like a rubber
moon to save me from severing

this crescent tongue
like a gutted fish.

And when the current flows,
I see a field of tiny clothes

the color of sun, buttons
double-stitched, legs blooming

out wide for fattened thighs.
I named her before

they could even say
that the cord we shared

snared her neck, starved her breath.
Shhhhh. My body doesn't know yet

that it's become a soilless grave.
Her headstone, her name

scrawled in blood on the sheets
of this asylum,

so when they wash them clean,
she'll be baptized with soap,

scoured with bleach.
And when I emerge shimmering

from this current to dry
under fluorescent light, it's likely

I'll forget—my heart is a pocket
heavy with stones sinking

every step, and because someone
had to cry, I've made a stream,

swift enough to swallow this lullaby,
cold enough to catch her

before the clock hums
for not just one, but two.

Decomposition

Begin with a white sheet of paper, pinch fingers and
thumb to shred thin colors for wings. There are no
scissors here, no sharp edges.

Squirt enough glue on one side to make certain
it will stick, check the flaps, the way the nurses
check under your tongue for wandering meds.
Chew a clump of hair free, delicately arrange as
feathers, something to coat the wiry bones for cold.
Color its loud, flapping soul a burnt red. Drop stars
like bird-scatter in the weedy lawn of sky. Trace the edges
dead black, dissect its parts with bars,

between the breast and the bowels. And if you forget
what a blackbird looks like, ask the nurses to spread
the curtains, look through your glass box as wing-beats
stutter, as wing-beats blink. Cough, as though you are
strangling its breath.

Common Room

Someone is turning off a light.
Someone else is working the rind free from its fruit.
Someone is slow-grinding in the doorframe, mouthing "plain, pain, pin, in,"
stripping letters away.
It's sexy and confining, profound and shameful in the same breath,
until it's not, until it's gray.
Someone is spread out on a couch, haphazard, elastic band tied around their arm.
Someone else is playing an imaginary piano and wiggling a decayed tooth.
Someone is dressing their wounds with words,
and the lights are on,
and the lights are off.

How to Snare a Wandering Womb

If discontent laces your skin,
scrawls your hair like a cup of ants
under heated glass,

if nerves take root as ache,
lines tissue and become the kind
of want that slicks a decent

wet between the soft
crevice of your sex while ironing
your husband's shirts, washing

dishes, or mending hems,
it can only mean that your womb
has packed the yellow Samsonite

bags you were saving for that
someday-cation and headed north
along the stony roads of your inner

route. That meddlesome bloat
is skirting outcropped ovaries,
straying the winding

maze of intestines, possibly
pausing to watch the blush-fat
nodes swell the horizon.

Remain calm. There's a cure
for such wanderlust, an olfactory
trick—a ceramic bowl

held under your nose,
a tincture so noxious it demands
the uterus reconsider

its chosen route, flee south.
A bowl of French lavender, vanilla,
or sage, straddled between legs,

the perfume of a debutante
to sweeten the lure of its descent.
Unless it bellowed loose during
a Valium dream

and is wandering the world
in search of a single blade

of grass to hold tightly,
so that when the wind stirs,
that whistle-song carries,

hums a lullaby of mislaid
ghosts, calls them back to roost,
it means you haven't been

diligent in keeping your body's promise.
The only thing it could reasonably desire
would be to stay filled.

Dogwood

The scars on my body
are burnt seeds—
scattered blooms
that singed in flame.

I thought once
I was a map of birch
and weed,
sinew
and milk,

that my breath began
the day we lay
in the field
palming blades of grass,

whistling from whispers,

ripping cerise flowers
from their stems.

You whispered so carefully,
this too I can include.

A field of lobbed flowers.
A tree of weeping sways.

Desire is a patch of scorched
earth that
never fully heals.

In the Waiting Room of the Earth Clinic

they have me stand against glass
to see the way my body reflects light.

The doctor rubs ash on my chest, slips it
deep in the creases of my hips, presses her small
hands to my low back, measures the needle-length
of my thready pulse.

There is such intense heat that I bellow and buck,
while she whispers to the spirit child that's nestled
between my ribs, like a craven bird.
She checks my tongue.

In the waiting room of the Earth Clinic,
I read the skin of the man next to me to kill time.
He holds his palms open, shows me his shins.
I let him trace the scar on my elbow where
I was hooked by a door hinge, straight through.

I'm called into a glass room so the doctor can see
the way my body reflects light, pain shadowing
the lithe bone-frame of wings that wrinkle and whisk
with each thrum of my heart.

She traces the shape with black ink, so she'll know
where to slip the knife.

Pen Pal, Asylum

I'm loose wires, twirls of yarn hair,
burnt-ash eyes swept from a stockroom floor.

I'm eighty percent paper, pink-thin skin,
litmus-blue for you.

Rub against my matchstick shin,
I'll ignite.

Wind me up, wind me up
take me for a ride.

My ragdoll lips are vigilant as vultures,
soft as weathered leather and chard.

My kiss is a spill of cumin on soft
bread, spongy warm, rising.

Some man patched my wounds
with slop from a bucket.

He milked me, swirled me,
spit me out.

Another man burnt buttons along my back
with his cigarette,

said he could see my spirit, like stuffing,
puffing out. I was his child-bride.

Now I'm yours to sew together,
your pile of groaning breasts and thighs,

a scabbed map of slices. You can split me
down my scar-lines. Shave me.

Save me. Shoot what you want
into my veins. I'm a cloud pocked with rain.
Wind me up, wind me up,
dig your hands into my spine.

I'll be your puppet, your glamour girl,
your bitch in heat, your insane.

I'll play twice-as-nice once the pills
float down this numb-ebbing wave.

I have time, so much time, for the fog
to burn off, the pollution to clear from my brain.

Can you hear the seagulls shriek *swallow, swallow,*
then check my tongue for a razor out of place?

(They have trust issues.) Come see.

Crank the bars from the glass. Free me.
I'll be your moon, your gun. Your edge to scratch on.

I'll write every day,
even though it's hard to know

which one becomes the last. The light
here shines fluorescent as the waxed floor.

Diagnosis

Listen, the story of our bodies
is splintered along this
cracked cup.

Take a sip, you'll
understand.

Hold the lifeline
of your palms open,

invite the wind
to juxtapose your longings

with kept secrets that have dissolved
like sugar into steaming Chai.

Look everywhere
for the thing you are not
missing.

Prairie Madness

I.

Grasshoppers,
like thick fingers
slapping the wind.

I walk among them,
a ghost displacing
little bodies at will.

II.

There are no edges
here, no sight-lines,
no sounds not swallowed
by the bursts of grit and
feathers of dust,

and the songbirds
that dare to winnow
forget one minute
from the last.

They hum spelt
memories without
so much as an echo
to blazon
something sharp.

III.

Their song is a string
looping my throat.

Their beaks are plows
pulling into the wind,
into the metal hardness of it,
the cold whistle beheading
any chance to bloom.

IV.

I boil tea
with dandelion
roots; even they
are wrinkled
with malaise.

V.

A woman could
rattle in such wide
spaces, hunted
by wings and wind.

VI.

I dream a mosaic
of centipede legs
and scorpion tails
leaking from walled
slabs of sod by my bed.

They chew my skin,
secrete my hair, nest
in my ears until the paper
clippings I hung begin
to cry.

VII.

There are no edges
here, no sight-lines,
no reasons why I'm
slipping to the side.

VIII.

If the wind stops
it's only to watch
a woman in flames
running headlong
for a stream,
a stream parched with silt.

III

In the Light of Morning

I make a camera with my hands.
My shutter-bug eyes clip the borders of your face,
brood-heavy, next to mine.

They frame a crack in the windowpane where the day
slips its early announcement.

I was away so long, listening to the scratch of indigo
birds that chirped on straw legs. It became my sorrow song.

The same cold light leaks over stacked papers, heaps of laundry
neglected to busy-living, as if to say *welcome home*.

I could wake up singing *I kiss the sky to send her blue a letter**,
but I know you've been worrying my name
in the dark. So I'll let you sleep.

When you wake, we'll sit by the heat of the oven,
dish the forensics of the day over coffee, sip errands,
fill forgotten histories.

It will feel like I never left.

Maybe we'll pretend it was only an afternoon,
that I was out back, tending the garden soil,
burying strands of hair I clipped
while you were tilling dreams.

---

*Paolo Nutini, "Better Man"

Harbinger

I stole the slingshot
from my brother's underwear drawer,

snapped it like a happy circumstance
at an oak flush with wings.

I won't lie. I loved the way
the sky clouded with bird-scatter—

intimate clumps of scared-shit drizzle
that splattered painted pavement

and the absolute quiet that can only follow
a full-sky frenzy.

It was as if the small bones of my chest
had shattered,

the way a store window can—slivers
sniping each direction, piercing flesh

with the precise amount of tenderness
it would take to stop a heart.

I Want to be Thrilled

the way my dog is,
sprinting through the pine bed
with a plump of plumage in her jaws.

I suggest a sky burial, but we toss
it in the trash with cardboard,
milk cartons, and soiled diapers,
most afraid of what it might attract.

Its eyes—the floaty windows—
were a liquid-film of scrambled yolk.

No thing left flapping there.

Only a drip of blood leaked
from its beak; breast so swollen
we knew its insides were jumbled into gunk.

A body of pulp and snagged sinew.
Dog-jowled feathers.

Its rubbery, limp feet— like any that tried
to grip into the shallow ground,
and at the same time, fly.

Sickness

It sours you like a cut,
pinches black licorice and gunmetal inside of your cheeks,
cinder-blocks legs like Orpheus, stumbling late to your bed,
looking you dead in the eye, smelling synthetic as cherry air-freshener
hanging from a taxicab mirror.
It charges you for distance while leaking lead into your limbs,
squints day through the blinds sharp as an inking needle
tattooing your eyelids,
and the squid of it all—
getting out of the tangle of blanket-weeds is as drag-foot
as trying to fly from the bottom of an algae-caked lake,
with one good push,
elbows first.

Tall Pines

Their needles drop
like barbed stars.

This late humidity
heavies the laundry
strung along the line.

Like bodies, after.

Like a whisper,
loud enough to wake
the starched earth,

its softening
this late in a season—
an answer
trying to swallow
scurrying
heels.

Needles stick into
my hair,

as if mine
is the breath that breaks
the coat of morning frost,

as if it's a choice
to trick
the inevitable
cold.

My Son Shakes a Small Rainmaker

The sound of rice scraping depressed wood
is the same music the tree outside is playing to the wind,
leaves brittled by a long winter.

His trilling becomes a prayer I taught him, to Ganesha,
only the words are too big for his mouth, so he sings
Jai Ganesha, om gum-gunna, gum-gunna
in its place.

I hear, tucked inside, a hollow rattle,
a metallic cold, the taste of tin.
I am eager for an early spring.

I Offer You This

You ask me to stand behind, stand in the etched quiet,
the imposed dark of your body.

I offer you this hyacinth, this string of paper lights,
because you have yet to ask about the shape of my heart.

I'll tell you.

The first time I saw antelope grazing, I stopped the car.
I watched the sure-footed way they roamed the dark.

I rolled down the glass, but still there was this separation.
My hand, extended, reaching from some far place inside.

Like the disembodied voice that streams the radio, the ache
that shadows ordinary words like rain, the soft crackle

before you pick up the phone, the words we've borrowed
that won't come close to describing grace, their softness,
in every way their not-humanness.

I've been told more than once that my best chance for surviving
any crash is to remain limp, unaffected, to imagine it's happening
to someone else, someone along the edges.

After, they will take a tally of injuries sustained, will record
gashes and breaks as if those are what keep us, are what keep
blood moving in, moving out.

My heart is not the quiet, the reaching, but the impulse
moments before, the bright smell of hyacinth that someone

removed from the room days ago. Fresh as echo.
Their wilt, sustained.

Building a Life from Sorrow

I chose instead to listen
to the birds and branches
creak under their slight
weight and warble,

the knocking woodpecker
who works without ever
expecting an answer,

and you, swinging that axe
over your right shoulder
with the kind of grace
that takes most men years
to arc into meditation.

This is the life we dreamt of living,
the one we trudged through
decades of rotted scraps to build.

Piece by piece you haul
and drop the split wood
into a neat pile at the steep
lip of the drive.

I know your secret.
You are building a wall,
one I'll be sure to notice
if I look in the rearview mirror.

On Your Sixth Birthday

Little egg, little cracked, white egg,
half-shell discarded on the pavement.

I lift it carefully with a stick, so the
cracks won't spider, so the whole-half

remains safe. I lift it to show you
something broke free today.

You peek inside, say
a caterpillar must have found his wings.

Elegy, Exhale

Someone told you that one day your voice will change,
little sparrow, little teardrop hammer in a tin bell,

and when brushing your teeth, a thin string of blood shapes
your gum-line, you discover that your first baby tooth

will soon leave too. How frightening the world must be at six,
how unsettling to be your bones, your palpitating dreams.

You still believe that I am the one who sends them nightly,
by pushing an invisible button between your eyes,

and how betrayed you must feel when you climb
next to the warmth of my body, disturbed by zombies,

flesh-colored sharks that are chasing you in sleep.
Forgive me, I've forgotten the need to mourn our fragile

losses, to give them names. Before you, there were two
that drowned in the folds of my body, no thicker than a palm print.

My bones, a graveyard of brattled dreams that forgot to bloom.
Someday, I will unearth the words to tell you, to teach you how

to celebrate the markings of growth—one heartbeat at a time.
But for now, let's dance. Let's lament, scuff a hole in the dirt,

swaddle our yesterdays in colored tissue, bury them under
the mantle of a crisp moon. If you want to sing, sing, little sparrow.

I'll let this breath catch in my throat, hold it there
until it feels full enough to release.

Little One

We curve our shadow-hands
into sparrows, send them soaring
over the tarmac of our dreams.

You grab my fingers, ask me to teach you
how to shape a gun on the blank wall.

Don't you just tip your peace fingers?

Point them like this.

Someday, mine will be the voice of reason
in your head. The ghosted mother.

A fractured poem. A cigarette hole.
A bearing.

We share secrets in the near-night
dim of the room. Mine. Yours.

Prayer for the Sick

My sweet boy
shits himself for six days.

I swaddle him in diapers,
even though he should be in school.

What sleep
comes in cracks between
large slabs of night—

cradling his sweat-blistered head,
soothing his febrile chatter,
helping him sit.

The small mechanics
he learned years ago, juddering now.

Open wide. I find myself pleading.
There's mush on this spoon—flake-white rice.
It will heal you.

I feel the squalor-grief of every dirt-caked
child with a plumped hunger belly,
of every mom with caked-dry breasts.

For a quarter a day.
But who is going to stop the flies?

Open wide. Please, open wide.
This warm snow will melt the moon.
Let it fill you.

I fear that if we pray, our pleas
will ache about the room,

useless as a yarn fly-swatter.

Mothering

The dishes pile like nosebleeds—
a sink of chipped blooms
waiting to be blotted.

I'm too tired to fuss,
or tidy.

I would rather unhinge
a cluster of violets from their roots—
growing lush in our septic field—

glue them into keepsake frames,

watch the gnats flicker from the underside of leaves
as they are trapped under glass.

Could they ever know the difference
between the overhead lamp
and sun?

Even the freezer surrenders its bulb-light
when left ajar
long enough.

This job requires
endless grafts to heal
skinned knees and tantrum-cuts.

I'm raw from splicing
tissue from my own damn heart.

Two-Lane Road, Tree

The crows are calling from the tree so loudly
that I'm sure they have our cat, bolts of tabby hair
sticking to their oily feathers, his pink-paper tongue
peek-a-booing from the side of a crooked beak.

They are raucous and vain in their lack of discrimination,
openly hunting death, shouting from the tree that it too
is insipid, a blood-gape with bone in the wound.
Only their language is as much warning as celebration,
mocking our denial that it can only end one way.

Winter

My winter hands smell like embers
that won't wash clean.

I'm spine-sore from carrying hefts of wood,
bending to the earth to gather kindling.

My children run in white-fall, shriek at the weight
that pulls thin limbs over their heads.

There's a scamper of tracks going out to the only
road that can take us; it, too, is a block of quiet.

The ice-glazed branches are paper letters that crack
in the wind. The dog, cozy by the fire, snarls at the

outside melt, ceremoniously nips at birds as they carry
shards and seeds that stick to folds of wet feathers.

The seeds lighten and drop—drop and bury deep
in knee-high drifts as the birds make their way, far.

Our breath makes a curtain we sleep under,
all of us tucked tightly in a row.

About the Author

Megan Merchant lives in the tall pines of Prescott, AZ. She is the author of two full-length poetry collections: *Gravel Ghosts* (Glass Lyre Press, Awarded 2016 Best Book Award), *The Dark's Humming* (Awarded 2015 Lyrebird Prize, Glass Lyre Press), four chapbooks, and a forthcoming children's book with Philomel Books. Most recently, she was the recipient of the 2016-2017 COG Literary Award, judged by Juan Felipe Herrera, U.S. Poet Laureate. She was also the recipient of the Las Vegas Poets Prize. You can find her work at meganmerchant.wix.com/poet.

Glass Lyre Press

exceptional works to replenish the spirit

Glass Lyre Press is an independent literary publisher interested in technically accomplished, stylistically distinct, and original work. Glass Lyre seeks diverse writers that possess a dynamic aesthetic and an ability to emotionally and intellectually engage a wide audience of readers.

Glass Lyre's vision is to connect the world through language and art. We hope to expand the scope of poetry and short fiction for the general reader through exceptionally well-written books, which evoke emotion, provide insight, and resonate with the human spirit.

Poetry Collections
Poetry Chapbooks
Select Short & Flash Fiction
Anthologies

www.GlassLyrePress.com

www.ingramcontent.com/pod-product-compliance
Lightning Source LLC
Chambersburg PA
CBHW021158080526
44588CB00008B/405